THE

SMARTPHONE

ENTREPRENEUR

Strategies for Building Wealth
Using Your Mobile Device

Norman M. Sanders

This book is a work of non-fiction and any resemblance to any persons, living or dead, or any events or occurrences, is purely coincidental. The characters and story lines are created from the author's imagination or are used fictitiously.

TABLE OF CONTENTS

INTRODUCTION

In the digital age we live in, mobile devices are an integral part of our daily lives. From managing schedules to connecting with others to running businesses, smartphones have revolutionized the way we work and interact. In today's world, entrepreneurship has become more accessible and attainable with the use of mobile devices. A new generation of entrepreneurs has emerged, known as the smartphone entrepreneurs. These entrepreneurs are leveraging the power of mobile technology to build and scale businesses, create wealth, and make an impact in their industries.

This book, "The Smartphone Entrepreneur: Strategies for Building Wealth Using Your

Mobile Device," is a comprehensive guide for anyone who wants to unlock the power of mobile entrepreneurship. In this book, you'll learn the fundamentals of entrepreneurship, how to develop business strategies using your smartphone, how to scale your business, and much more. You'll also gain valuable insights into how the mobile landscape is changing and shaping the future of entrepreneurship.

We believe that mobile entrepreneurship has the power to change lives and communities. By reading this book, you'll be equipped with the knowledge and tools to become a successful smartphone entrepreneur, making a positive impact and building the wealth you deserve.

CHAPTER 1:

UNDERSTANDING ENTREPRENEURSHIP

Entrepreneurship is the art of creating and managing a business venture, and it's a critical facet of modern economic life. As a smartphone entrepreneur, understanding the core tenets of entrepreneurship is essential to growing a successful business.

1. What is Entrepreneurship? The chapter starts by exploring what exactly entrepreneurship is and what it entails. It's not just about creating a business; it also involves taking calculated risks, developing creative solutions, building a team, and executing plans effectively. Understanding

what entrepreneurship is and isn't is critical to creating a solid business foundation.

2. Qualities of Entrepreneurs: Understanding the qualities of successful entrepreneurs is the next essential step for the smartphone entrepreneur. Entrepreneurs need to have specific traits and attributes, including creativity, resilience, leadership, problem-solving abilities, and adaptability. As a smartphone entrepreneur, possessing these competencies will help you stay competitive in the marketplace and navigate uncertainty.

3. Types of Entrepreneurship: One misconception about entrepreneurship is that it only involves developing a product or service from scratch. However, there are

different types of entrepreneurship. These include technology entrepreneurship, social entrepreneurship, and lifestyle entrepreneurship. Understanding the differences between these will help you identify your strengths and weaknesses and make informed decisions about the type of business to pursue.

4. Goal-Setting and Planning Setting realistic goals that align with your business vision is crucial for a smartphone entrepreneur. The chapter will explore how to create SMART goals that are specific, measurable, attainable, relevant, and time-bound. Additionally, creating a solid business plan with concrete steps to achieving those goals is critical for successful entrepreneurship.

5. Financial Management: The chapter will also explain how to manage finances successfully as a smartphone entrepreneur. Understanding financial statements, developing an accounting system, and basic financial management strategies will help you make informed decisions about pricing and budgeting.

6. Leadership and Teamwork: Finally, we'll explore how to build a strong team that will help you achieve your business goals and objectives. This includes how to develop leadership skills, how to communicate effectively with diverse teams, and how to navigate conflict. With mobility, you can coordinate and collaborate with various team members globally.

In summary, understanding entrepreneurship as a smartphone entrepreneur helps you develop and implement business strategies that will create wealth for yourself. Understanding what entrepreneurship is, the qualities possessed by entrepreneurs, the different types, successful goal-setting and planning, financial management, leadership, and teamwork are all vital components of entrepreneurial success in the digital age.

CHAPTER 2:

BENEFITS OF ENTREPRENEURSHIP

Entrepreneurship is not just a way to earn a living; it's a lifestyle that offers many unique advantages. In this chapter, we will delve deeper into the benefits of entrepreneurship, particularly with regard to being a smartphone entrepreneur.

1. Financial Benefits: The financial benefits of entrepreneurship are numerous, including the potential for higher income and wealth creation. As a smartphone entrepreneur, you have the advantage of low overhead and the ability to tap into a global market. This can generate a higher income than a traditional

job and provide more financial security. Additionally, entrepreneurship offers significant tax advantages, including the ability to write off business expenses such as technology, workspace, and travel.

2. Personal Benefits: Entrepreneurship can also offer numerous personal benefits, including the ability to work on passion projects. As a smartphone entrepreneur, you can build a business around something you love and enjoy working on every day. This creates a sense of fulfillment that is unmatched by traditional employment. With entrepreneurship, you also have the autonomy to make decisions and take on new challenges, which deepens your sense of purpose and motivates continued growth.

3. Social Benefits: Entrepreneurship also offers unique social benefits, particularly with regard to being a smartphone entrepreneur. You can create jobs, contribute to your local community, and make an impact on society. The rise of mobile applications and the internet has made entrepreneurship more accessible, which has had a democratizing effect on the economy. You can leverage technology to provide services or products that will make life more convenient for other people.

4. Specific Benefits of Smartphone Entrepreneurship: What separates smartphone entrepreneurship from other types of entrepreneurship is the convenience factor. With the rise of mobile applications, you can work from anywhere at any time, as

long as you have your mobile device. This allows for a flexible work-life balance that many traditional jobs don't provide. Additionally, utilizing your mobile device for business operations is often much more cost-effective compared to traditional equipment, thus creating a high return on investment relative to other industries.

In summary, entrepreneurship offers many benefits that go beyond financial gain, including personal and social fulfillment. And within the world of entrepreneurship, the smartphone entrepreneur specifically has the unprecedented convenience factor to help streamline, manage, and achieve all goals in building a business and creating wealth.

CHAPTER 3:

TYPES OF ENTREPRENEURSHIP

The previous chapter covered the basics of entrepreneurship and what it takes to be a successful smartphone entrepreneur. In this chapter, we'll delve deeper into the different types of entrepreneurship and how they apply to the smartphone entrepreneur.

1. Technology Entrepreneurship: Technology entrepreneurship involves creating a business based on innovative technological ideas or inventions. These businesses focus on developing new technology or improving existing technology to solve real-world problems. As

a smartphone entrepreneur, there are many opportunities in the technology sector, whether it's creating a new app, developing a digital platform, or improving existing technology. Technology entrepreneurship can be both exciting and profitable for smartphone entrepreneurs who want to create something new and innovative.

2. Social Entrepreneurship: Social entrepreneurship involves creating a business that's focused on solving social problems or making a positive impact on society. These businesses are often mission-driven and have a long-term goal of making a positive difference in the world. As a smartphone entrepreneur, you can leverage technology to create a social impact, whether it's by creating an app that

helps people in vulnerable situations, using digital marketing to create awareness about a social issue, or using social media to advocate for a cause. Social entrepreneurship is a rewarding and fulfilling type of entrepreneurship for smartphone entrepreneurs who want to make a positive impact on society.

3. Lifestyle Entrepreneurship: Lifestyle entrepreneurship is a type of entrepreneurship that focuses on creating a business around an individual's personal interests or hobbies. These businesses are often centered on the passions, hobbies, or interests of the smartphone entrepreneur and usually provide a good work-life balance. As a smartphone entrepreneur, you can create a business that aligns with your

personal interests, whether it's creating a fashion app or developing a lifestyle coaching service. Lifestyle entrepreneurship is a great opportunity for smartphone entrepreneurs who are seeking financial freedom while pursuing their passions.

4. Franchise Entrepreneurship: Franchise entrepreneurship involves running a business under a pre-established brand name or parent company. As a franchisee, you benefit from an established brand, support from the parent company, and a proven business model. As a smartphone entrepreneur, there are many franchise opportunities that you can take advantage of, whether it's in the food industry or in retail. Franchise entrepreneurship offers a level of

security and predictability that other types of entrepreneurship may not offer.

In summary, the smartphone entrepreneur has a range of entrepreneurial opportunities, whether creating innovative products or services, solving social issues through technology, building a business around a passion-based lifestyle, or taking advantage of existing brands and franchising. Each option has its own unique advantages and challenges and requires different strategies and skills, so it's important to do your research and make informed decisions that align with your strengths, interests, and goals.

CHAPTER 4:

THE MOBILE BUSINESS LANDSCAPE

The Mobile Business Landscape focuses on the various ways to make money through mobile business initiatives. There are many different ways to monetize mobile phones, from creating and selling applications to offering services such as marketing or consulting.

The most popular and easiest way to monetize a mobile device is to create and sell apps. Apps are the most downloaded and purchased items on mobile devices, so developing and marketing an app will be a great way to quickly create a profitable mobile business. The key to success in this arena is to choose the right app concept and develop an app that is both engaging and of high quality. Mobile app development also requires a significant amount of knowledge of the development process, so it's important to understand the basics of app development before attempting to create an app.

In addition to apps, you can also use your mobile device to offer services such as consulting and marketing. Offering services on a mobile device allows you to reach a larger pool of customers that would otherwise not be able to access your services on a traditional laptop or desktop. For example, you can use your mobile device to offer digital marketing services, such as helping businesses create and execute successful digital campaigns.

You can also use your mobile phone to sell products or promote other businesses. With the help of near-field communication (NFC) technology, consumers may send money using their smartphones, enabling you to open an online store and sell goods or advertise for other companies. You can also use your mobile device to advertise other businesses, such as restaurants or hotels, as well as your own services and products.

Finally, you can use your mobile phone as a platform for mobile payments. With mobile payment services, you can easily accept payments for services from customers. You can also use mobile payments to accept donations for charities or provide payment services to other businesses.

These are just a few of the many ways to monetize a mobile device. With the right strategy and the right knowledge, you can quickly develop a profitable mobile business.

CHAPTER 5:

MOBILE APP DEVELOPMENT AND DESIGN

When it comes to mobile app development and design, there are a few key steps that all entrepreneurs should take to ensure their success. Entrepreneurs need to understand the entire development and design process, from conceptualizing their idea to picking the right platform to development and launch.

1. Conceptualize Your App Ideas

The first step in mobile app development and design is to conceptualize your ideas. What do you want the app to accomplish? What features do you need or want? Figuring out the concept and purpose of your app will help you decide the next step: which platform to choose.

2. Choose a Platform

Choosing the best platform for your app is crucial. Your choice will depend on your target audience and the device they are using. There are two main platforms, iOS (Apple) and Android (Google), and each has its own development and design process.

3. Development

The development process for both iOS and Android involves creating the app architecture, coding the user interface, and then finally programming the app's features. You'll work more quickly and have a better understanding of the development process if you have a fundamental understanding of the coding language and development framework.

4. Design

Your app design will affect the user experience, and it is important to create a thoughtful and engaging one. The design elements include creating the user interface, picking the right color palette, and using the right fonts and typography. It is important to create a seamless design for the user that is both pleasing and functional.

5. Testing and Release

Before releasing the app, it is important to do a test run and make sure it is ready for the market. Testing the app is essential to fixing any bugs or errors that may occur. After the testing phase is complete, the app should be ready to launch.

With the right strategy, an understanding of the development and design processes, and a bit of luck, your mobile app can be a success! People can make money from apps in various ways, such as by selling virtual goods, offering subscription services, and placing ads. Developing a mobile app may seem daunting, but with the right focus and planning, you can be a successful smartphone entrepreneur.

CHAPTER 6:

MOBILE PAYMENT SYSTEMS

Mobile payment systems (MPS) have become increasingly popular in the past few years due to their convenience and accessibility to everyday consumers.

Not only are they becoming increasingly popular, but they also provide entrepreneurs with an opportunity to make money through the design and implementation of the payment system. This chapter will discuss the importance of creating an MPS, the benefits of using one, and the components that help create a mobile payment system.

An MPS is beneficial for many reasons and is becoming increasingly popular due to its enhanced user experience, lower transaction costs, and increased security.

In addition to all of these benefits, an MPS offers entrepreneurs an opportunity to make money. An entrepreneur can create a payment system by researching the market, focusing on the customer's needs, and integrating the technology. Researching the market is an important step in order to determine the best way to provide a versatile payment platform. This requires an entrepreneur to understand the needs of their customers in order to develop a payment platform that is efficient, secure, and meets their needs.

Once the research has been completed, the technology must be integrated into the system. The technology should include an encryption algorithm that protects customers' data from theft.

Additionally, the MPS should include a payment gateway that allows users to securely make payments through the platform. Other components that may also be necessary include a merchant processor, software development, an automated receipting system, and a payment analytics system.

In addition to the technology that is needed to build an MPS, an entrepreneur may need to partner with a payment processor. This will enable an entrepreneur to make money from online and mobile transactions. The payment processor takes a percentage of each payment, which can be a substantial income for the entrepreneur. Additionally, the entrepreneur should consider implementing different incentives and offers that will attract customers to use the payment platform.

Furthermore, the entrepreneur should consider marketing strategies that will help promote the payment platform. The most effective way to market the payment platform is through social media channels, such as Facebook and Twitter.

Additionally, it is important to be active on the platform and provide content that serves the meme and encourages others to support the platform.

In conclusion, building a mobile payment system is an opportunity to make money and provide customers with efficient and secure transactions. The technology must be integrated, and a payment processor must be partnered with it in order to be successful. Furthermore, marketing strategies must be developed to promote the payment platform. With the right approach and dedication from the entrepreneur, a MPS can be a successful venture.

CHAPTER 7:

SOCIAL MEDIA AND MARKETING TECHNIQUES

Social media and marketing are two topics that cannot go together these days, and the idea of making money through them has become popular in modern society. Therefore, it is essential for entrepreneurs to understand the importance of these marketing techniques and how to leverage the potential of digital marketing to make money.

The key to success with social media marketing is to establish yourself as an authority and influencer. A well-crafted social media strategy helps not only to raise brand awareness but also to reach potential customers, build relationships, and establish trust. Engage with your audience and post content that is relevant to them. For example, if you are selling clothing, post videos of how to style certain items or compare the different makes and models. When customers feel like they are getting more than just a sales pitch, they are more likely to make a purchase.

It is important to make sure you are targeting the right audience when using social media to market. Different platforms can be used to reach people from different backgrounds, so it is essential to use the right platforms for your business. For example, if you are targeting a young demographic, you may opt for Instagram and TikTok. On the other hand, LinkedIn may be a better platform for a business focused on a more professional audience.

Creating and growing an audience also helps to make money, as you can use it to build relationships, increase visibility for your products or services, and ultimately drive sales. Growing an audience requires more than just posting relevant content; it also requires engaging with the audience and responding to their comments. Also, look for opportunities to collaborate with influencers who already have a large following. This can help to further increase your exposure and build your business.

Another important tip for making money through social media is to drive organic traffic to your website or other online platforms. This can be done through smart and creative content marketing strategies, such as creating blogs or videos that provide useful information. This can generate interest in your business, leading your customers to seek out your products or services. Lastly, building a loyal following through rewards and promotions can further increase sales and increase your chances of making money with social media.

To sum up, social media marketing and techniques are essential for entrepreneurs who want to make money with their smartphones. It is important to create an effective strategy, target the right audience, increase visibility, develop relationships, and create organic traffic. If done properly, social media can be an effective tool to drive sales and increase income.

CHAPTER 8:

SETTING UP A BUSINESS ON YOUR SMARTPHONE

Most entrepreneurs aspire to be able to run successful businesses on their own. With the advances in modern technology, entrepreneurs now have the tools within their reach to do just that—through smartphones.

Setting up a business on your smartphone is a relatively straightforward process. The first step is to choose the right type of business. Mobile businesses—including blogging, social media, coding, or app development—are all great options. The key is to choose something that plays to your strengths.

Once you have chosen what type of business you want to do, the next step is to take advantage of the many available mobile tools and apps that can help you get your business up and running. Some of the more popular ones include scheduling software, invoicing, accounting, payment systems, CRMs, and other software.

In addition to the apps themselves, there are plenty of resources for advice and guidance. Podcasts and websites are filled with tips on getting started as a business, small business marketing, developing apps, and more. You can also seek business mentorship from other entrepreneurs or seek out a business coach to help you find success in your entrepreneurial journey.

The most important part of setting up a business on your smartphone is identifying a target market. Knowing who you are serving and what types of needs your business can fill will be essential to making sure your business is successful. Take time to research your market, understand their needs, and develop a product or service that they are willing to pay for.

Finally, you need to establish your digital presence. Make sure you have a website, blog, and social media presence so that you can promote your business and offer it to your target audience. Once you have created an online presence, you need to focus on how you are going to make money. This may include creating a subscription-based product or service, charging for consulting services, or becoming an affiliate marketer.

Overall, setting up a business on your smartphone is an exciting yet daunting task. The great news is that there are plenty of resources and tools available to help entrepreneurs succeed. The key is to find the right fit, make sure you fully understand your target market, and develop a product or service they will not only need but also be able to afford. With a clear plan and the right tools, you can create your own successful business.

CHAPTER 9:

BUILDING A MOBILE BUSINESS MODEL

Mobile technology has become an integral part of the modern business world, making it easier and more efficient for entrepreneurs to manage their businesses. It's now easier than ever for entrepreneurs to build their own mobile business models using their smartphones.

Using a mobile business model with a smartphone allows entrepreneurs to quickly and efficiently manage their business operations, keep in touch with their customers, and stay on top of their competitors. With the right tools and strategies, entrepreneurs can take advantage of mobile technology to build a successful business on their own smartphones.

The first step in creating a successful mobile business model is researching the market and understanding your target customers. It's critical to understand your target market and what types of customers you need to target in order to make the most of your mobile business. Knowing who your target customers are and what they want will help entrepreneurs develop effective strategies for acquiring and retaining customers.

Once you know who your target customers are, entrepreneurs can begin to focus on developing their mobile business plan. A good mobile business plan should include a marketing strategy, a development plan, and a budget. The marketing strategy should focus on how to acquire and retain customers in order to maximize profits. The development plan should cover the costs and resources required for developing and launching the business model. Finally, the budget should reflect the resources and expenses associated with the business.

To effectively launch a business model using a smartphone, entrepreneurs need to set up their mobile business. This involves creating a website, registering a domain name, and setting up an online store. These steps are necessary for entrepreneurs to efficiently manage their business operations.

After entrepreneurs have set up their mobile businesses, they need to create marketing campaigns tailored for mobile users. Calculated campaigns will make it easier for entrepreneurs to acquire and retain customers. A good marketing strategy should focus on how to reach potential customers and target their market segment with the right content.

Once entrepreneurs have acquired customers through their marketing efforts, they need to focus on providing excellent customer service. This involves understanding customer needs and providing them with helpful customer support. The key here is to make sure that customers are satisfied with the service and products provided, as this will be key to building a successful business model.

Finally, entrepreneurs need to track their mobile business performance and analyze the results. Understanding which marketing campaigns are working and which are not will enable entrepreneurs to increase their profitability.

In conclusion, entrepreneurs can use their smartphones to easily launch their own business models. With the right tools and strategies, entrepreneurs can create effective mobile business models.

CHAPTER 10:
CREATING A MOBILE BUSINESS PLAN, STRATEGY AND EXECUTION.

The advent of today's "smartphone" technology presents a unique opportunity for formulating plans and strategies to create a mobile business. By understanding the basic principles of mobile business, app development, and marketing, entrepreneurs can develop strategies to make money on their smartphones. This chapter will explore how to create an effective mobile business plan, strategy, and execution for making money using a smartphone.

Creating an Effective Mobile Business Plan

The first step in creating a mobile business is to develop an effective plan. This includes developing an idea for a product or service, understanding the target market, and determining a pricing strategy.

It is important to consider how to promote the app and build a strong user base in order to maximize potential sales. It is also important to consider the financial implications and potential sustainability of the business before launching.

A thorough plan must provide detailed steps to launch the product or service, create visibility for the product, generate revenue, and grow the customer base.

Developing the Mobile Strategy

Once the mobile business plan is complete, entrepreneurs must develop a strategy that will ensure the product's success. This strategy should include the steps required to develop the app and the necessary engineering and coding skills involved. It is important to consider the platform being used, as different operating systems have different user interfaces. Quality assurance must also be considered to ensure reliable performance and create a positive user experience. Marketing plans must be developed, including detailed strategies on how to build awareness and generate organic traffic for the app.

Executing the Plan

The last step in creating a mobile business is to execute the plan. This involves making the necessary investments in equipment, software, and personnel to develop and launch the product. Once the product is ready for launch, the marketing plan must be executed. This includes setting up the product page, advertising, and working with influencers to promote the product. Once the product is live, it is important to monitor user engagement and continuously provide updates and improvements.

Creating a mobile business requires an effective plan, strategy, and execution in order to be successful. By understanding the basic principles of mobile business, app development, and marketing, entrepreneurs can develop strategies to make money on their smartphones. By investing time and resources into creating an effective plan to maximize sales potential and understanding the necessary marketing tactics to build visibility, entrepreneurs can create success in the mobile business.

CHAPTER 11:

TOOLS AND TECHNIQUES FOR MOBILE BUSINESS MANAGEMENT

The mobile revolution is transforming the way businesses are managed. For entrepreneurs keen on staying ahead of the curve, staying current with the latest tools and techniques for mobile business management is vital. By integrating technology into business processes, entrepreneurs can maximize efficiency, improve customer service, and increase profits. The Smartphone Entrepreneur: Strategies for Building Wealth Using Your Mobile Device is a valuable resource for those looking to stay up-to-date and on the cutting edge.

Tools and Techniques for Mobile Business Management provides an in-depth examination of the top resources available to increase profitability and efficiency. From software and apps to develop and monitor inventories to cloud-based business management services, entrepreneurs can find the right tool to meet their objectives.

Software and Apps:

One of the most valuable tools for mobile business management is mobile applications and software. This software provides the ability to organize and manage business operations right from a mobile device. Claims management software, such as

Cloverly, allows entrepreneurs to handle customer claims directly from their phones.

Inventory tracking and management apps, such as Provenience, provide the ability to track and update inventory levels in real time. This is especially crucial for businesses dealing with perishable goods. Accounting software, such as Intuit QuickBooks, allows entrepreneurs to keep track of invoices, expenses, accounts receivable, taxes, and more. These apps can be accessed from any location, giving entrepreneurs greater control and flexibility over their business operations.

Cloud-Based Business Management Services:

Cloud-based business management services are becoming increasingly popular with entrepreneurs. It provides a secure and easy-to-use platform to manage and store data. Services such as Microsoft Office 365 and Google Suite allow entrepreneurs to manage files, contacts, calendars, and project tasks from their mobile devices.

For entrepreneurs looking for more than just data storage, a full-featured business management solution, such as Microsoft Dynamics 365, can provide the comprehensive features needed for business growth and success. This platform allows entrepreneurs to access all their business information in one place, with features such as customer relationship management, sales automation, and analytics.

Social Media:

Social media is another indispensable tool for mobile business management. Social media platforms, such as Facebook and Instagram, allow entrepreneurs to reach new customers, engage with existing ones, and build a stronger brand. Entrepreneurs can create their own profiles and/or pages to promote their businesses. Through these profiles, entrepreneurs can share updated information and announcements, showcase the products and services they offer, and establish a presence in the community.

For entrepreneurs to successfully maximize profits and improved efficacy, having the right tool for the job is essential. Every business has different needs, Choosing the best mobile business management system is so crucial. Whether it's mobile applications, cloud-based services, or utilizing social media, having the right tool in place can prove to be invaluable when it comes to the success of a business.

CHAPTER 12:

LEGAL AND ETHICAL ISSUES IN MOBILE BUSINESS

Smartphone entrepreneurs need to be aware of the legal and ethical issues associated with mobile businesses. This chapter will focus on the legal and ethical issues that come up, how to ensure that your mobile business is compliant with all necessary laws, and how to be an ethical mobile entrepreneur. The goal of this chapter is to provide smartphone entrepreneurs with the knowledge and tools to help them make smart decisions and stay abreast of the latest legal and ethical standards for their mobile businesses.

Legal issues

The legal issues associated with mobile businesses can vary greatly depending on your business model, location, and industry. It's important to keep up with changes in the law and be aware of any relevant regulations and requirements.

Data privacy and protection laws

Data privacy laws protect consumers' personal information from being misused and abused by businesses. All mobile businesses should adhere to data privacy laws by requiring customers to consent to the business collecting and using personal data and by only collecting the necessary data for the purposes of the business. It is also important to ensure that data is securely stored and only accessed by authorized personnel.

Government regulations

Government regulations can vary significantly depending on the industry or business type. For example, businesses in the healthcare sector must comply with the Health Insurance Portability and Accountability Act (HIPAA) as well as the US Food and Drug Administration (FDA) regulations. Smartphone entrepreneurs should make sure to comply with all relevant regulations before launching their mobile businesses.

Licensing and permits

Licensing and permits can be required for mobile businesses, depending on the type of services being offered and the jurisdiction. For example, businesses offering financial services must have a valid license from their state's banking regulator. It's important to research the state and local laws in your area to determine if any particular licenses or permits are required.

Taxes

Taxes are an important consideration for any business, mobile or otherwise. Mobile businesses must pay taxes on income earned as well as any applicable sales taxes. It's important to research and understand the rules and regulations surrounding taxes on a local, state, and federal level so that you can ensure that your business is in compliance with all laws.

Ethical issues

In addition to complying with the relevant laws, mobile businesses should also strive to adhere to a set of ethical standards. This includes being transparent with customers and employees about data or business practices, treating customers fairly and with respect, and avoiding any deceptive or exploitative business practices.

Data collection and use

Mobile businesses should be transparent about the type of data they collect and how it is used. Customers should be informed of what data is being collected, how it is used, and the purpose of the data. Additionally, it is important to ensure that data is securely stored and not shared or sold to third parties without permission.

Consumer protection

It's also important for mobile businesses to ensure that they are treating their customers fairly. This includes honoring any warranties or guarantees they may offer, providing accurate information about products or services, and taking steps to prevent any deceptive or exploitative practices.

Workplace ethics

Mobile businesses should also strive to have a workplace that reflects a set of ethical standards. This includes providing employees with a safe working environment, respecting their rights, and ensuring that employees are paid equitably. Additionally, there should be a set of procedures in place for handling complaints and grievances.

Mobile businesses have to deal with a variety of legal and ethical considerations. From data privacy and government regulations to workplace ethics and consumer protection, it is important for smartphone entrepreneurs to understand the relevant laws and ethical standards in order to stay compliant and ensure that their mobile business is operating ethically. By taking the necessary steps to understand the legal and ethical issues associated with mobile business, smartphone entrepreneurs can have a successful and sustainable business.

CHAPTER 13:

SECURITY IN MOBILE BUSINESS

Mobile business owners face the challenge of securing their data while conducting their everyday operations. Businesses are more vulnerable to security breaches when dealing with mobile devices due to their portability and the fact that they can be used to access confidential or customer data. As such, it is essential to take the necessary steps to protect business data and transactions on mobile devices.

One of the first steps to secure mobile business is the establishment of a secure connection between an individual's business device and their home office or other office establishments. Mobile device owners should strongly focus on the development of secure wi-fi networks to protect the data and activities held on their devices from potential hackers. Utilization of WPA2 encryption technology is a must if any secure connection is to be established or maintained. Similarly, implementing robust Virtual Private Network (VPN) protocols is also advisable to ensure secure data transmission and reduce the risks associated with cyber-attacks.

In addition to protecting the device's connection, mobile business owners should implement similar security measures on their mobile devices. This includes the recommended use of finger print or facial recognition measures as two-factor authentication for the device, as well as the consideration of VPNs when accessing sensitive items, such as customer financial, health, and personal information. Moreover, the integration of a mobile device management (MDM) platform is essential for remote device access and management and for helping to preserve the device's security. Functions such as software installation and the enforcement of complex passwords can be established through the integration of an MDM platform.

Mobile applications can also be used to further protect data while conducting business activities. These applications, such as geo-fencing and anti-theft software, allow an individual to protect the device from potential theft and malicious activity. Similarly, firewalls and antivirus programs are essential for protecting the device against malware activity. Lastly, mobile devices should never be left unsupervised, especially not in areas that are vulnerable to theft.

In conclusion, the security of mobile businesses is essential to protect the data and activities conducted on the device. To do so, mobile device owners should ensure the implementation of secure connections between the device and the home or office premises. Security measures, such as two-factor authentication, VPNs, and MDM platforms, should be put in place on the device itself to help reduce the risk of cyberattacks. The integration of geo-fencing and anti-theft software, as well as firewalls and antivirus programs, is also essential for the device's protection. Lastly, personal vigilance is strongly advised when leaving the device in common or vulnerable areas.

CHAPTER 14:

AVOIDING BURNOUT IN MOBILE ENTREPRENEURSHIP

Mobile entrepreneurs have the advantage of having the freedom to work from wherever they choose. However, they can also be vulnerable to burnout if they do not take steps to manage their stress levels. Burnout can have a negative impact on both physical and mental health and can lead to reduced productivity and decreased motivation. This chapter focuses on the importance of recognizing the signs of burnout and taking proactive steps to prevent it.

The first step in preventing burnout is to understand the causes. Stress is the primary cause of burnout and can be caused by a variety of factors, including tight deadlines, a lack of control over projects, feeling overwhelmed, and uncertainty about the future. In addition, burnout can be caused by feelings of being unappreciated, a lack of feedback, and long hours without breaks.

It is important for mobile entrepreneurs to recognize the signs of burnout so that they can take steps to prevent it. Symptoms can include increased fatigue, irritability, decreased motivation, and a lack of enthusiasm. Other physical symptoms can include headaches, digestive problems, and insomnia.

One of the most effective strategies for preventing burnout is to create a healthy work-life balance. This means setting aside time for activities outside of work, such as exercise, hobbies, or spending time with family. It is also important to make sure that you take regular breaks during the day to give yourself time to relax and recharge.

It can also be helpful to delegate tasks and focus on what is important. This can help prevent feeling overwhelmed and give you the chance to focus on the most important tasks. When possible, it is also beneficial to collaborate with others on projects to reduce the amount of work that needs to be done. It can also be helpful to make sure that you are taking the time to recognize your achievements and celebrate them.

Setting clear boundaries is another important step in preventing burnout. This means determining when you are available and not letting clients or coworkers intrude on your time. It can also be beneficial to practice healthy time management and prioritize tasks. Time management techniques can help you better organize your tasks so that you can focus on the most important ones.

Mobile entrepreneurs should also practice self-care to help prevent burnout. This includes eating a healthy diet, getting enough sleep, and taking breaks for exercise or relaxation. It is also important to limit the amount of alcohol and caffeine that you consume and to make sure that you have enough social support.

Finally, it is important for mobile entrepreneurs to look for signs of burnout and take steps to prevent it. This means recognizing symptoms and taking the necessary steps to address them, such as setting clear boundaries, creating a healthy work-life balance, and practicing self-care. By using these strategies, mobile entrepreneurs can ensure that they are not becoming victims of burnout.

CHAPTER 15: DETERMINING WHEN TO SCALE YOUR MOBILE BUSINESS AND STRATEGIES FOR SCALING A MOBILE BUSINESS

The Smartphone Entrepreneur has highlighted the importance of scaling a mobile business for increased success. Chapter 16 serves to introduce entrepreneurs to the concept of assessing when to scale and the strategies required to scale a mobile business.

Scaling is defined as "the process of expanding an existing business as a means of increasing its potential for growth and profitability. It involves adding new products or services, introducing customer segments to new markets, or entering into partnerships or agreements with other companies" (Baker & Associates, 2016). As such, typically, when it comes to scaling a mobile business, it involves expanding the scope of the business, which includes the products and/or services, the customer segments, and/or the overall markets in which the business serves.

Knowing when to scale is an important part of a business's life cycle, as this could make or break its future success. In order to determine when to scale, it is important to consider a multitude of factors such as customer demand, business sustainability, market analysis, customer feedback, competition, the scalability of the current business model, and so on. The bottom line is that a business cannot scale if it has not successfully proven itself in the current market, so this is the foundation for any successful scaling endeavor.

Once a business is deemed ready to scale, strategies for doing so must be employed in order to ensure success. Business owners should consider the following strategies when scaling their mobile business:

• Establish new partnerships: In order to scale successfully, it is important to leverage the resources of other businesses or organizations. This could include building strategic alliances, forming joint ventures, outsourcing services, and more. Partnering with other businesses provides the opportunity to reach new customers, open new markets, and increase overall revenue and profits.

• Invest in SEO: Organic search engine optimization (SEO) helps increase the visibility of a mobile business online. Through SEO tactics and optimization, businesses can reach potential customers more quickly, resulting in increased sales and profits.

• Utilize social media: social media platforms offer a wide reach for those with even the smallest of budgets. Utilizing social media as a marketing tool increases the visibility and reach of a business by allowing it to engage with potential customers, provide value and content, and allow for easy feedback and communication. By leveraging social media in the scaling of a mobile business, potential customers are reached more quickly and effectively.

• Develop an App: With the current surge in mobile usage, it is paramount for both existing and scaling businesses to have an app. This allows a potential customer to easily access the business and utilize it while providing increased visibility and reach to the business, generating more opportunities for customers.

- Utilize data analytics: Data and analytics can offer invaluable insights into the performance and health of a business. Analytics allows a business to better understand its customers, market landscape, and potential expansion opportunities.

These strategies, when employed properly and in conjunction with one another, allow businesses to scale successfully. However, it is important to remember that scaling is a delicate process that could easily result in failure if not approached and implemented properly. The key to success is to ensure a clear understanding of the goals and strategies to be employed, customer and market analysis, and the development and adherence to a comprehensive plan.

Ultimately, scaling a mobile business is not a simple process and definitely requires time and resources, but it could bring a multitude of benefits when done correctly. The strategies outlined above are essential to ensuring the most successful scaling experience for any mobile business.

CHAPTER 16:

CHALLENGES AND OPPORTUNITIES IN SCALING A MOBILE BUSINESS

In an increasingly digital age, businesses are looking for ways to create the best and most efficient customer experience. Mobile technology has been both a blessing and a curse, as it has enabled businesses to connect with customers faster and more frequently than ever but also presents unique challenges. In the book "The Smartphone Entrepreneur: Strategies for Building Wealth Using Your Mobile Device," chapter eighteen discusses the unique challenges and opportunities that come with scaling a mobile business.

In order to successfully scale a mobile business, entrepreneurs must be prepared to adapt and grow with changing technology and customer requirements.

One of the major obstacles entrepreneurs face when scaling their mobile businesses is the ever-changing technological landscape. Growth in mobile technology has been incredibly fast, which makes it difficult to keep up with the latest trends. The mobile entrepreneur must be able to quickly adapt to the new technologies, applications, and features available in the mobile space.

Another difficulty often encountered when scaling a mobile business is the cost associated with purchasing new hardware and software. Mobile platforms come with a lot of upfront costs as well as ongoing expenses for maintenance and updates. Additionally, the cost of marketing and advertising campaigns can be significant, depending on the scope of the campaign. Therefore, entrepreneurs must decide on both the quantity and type of investment required to scale their mobile business.

It's crucial to keep in mind that scaling a mobile business involves both improving the customer experience and expanding client reach. The mobile entrepreneur must strive to make the experience customer-centered and focus on creating an engaging experience that meets the customer's needs. This requires staying up-to-date with the latest mobile trends and tools so that users have the most satisfactory experience.

Successfully scaling a mobile business also demands an understanding of the unique consumer behavior in the mobile space. Mobile consumers often conduct their searches differently than traditional web users, have different expectations, and are more likely to encounter problems with such an intuitive, easy-to-use experience. Therefore, entrepreneurs must be aware of these differences and develop strategies to ensure customers have the best experience possible.

The key to scaling a successful mobile business is thoughtful and tailored planning. The entrepreneur must take into account any and all available resources, including financial resources, human resources, and technological resources. Additionally, the entrepreneur must consider any potential barriers, such as legal or regulatory restrictions, as well as possible risks, such as data security. Finally, the entrepreneur needs to have a solid understanding of the current mobile market, the latest trends in the space, and any developments that have the potential to disrupt their business model.

Overall, mobile business owners have a unique set of challenges and opportunities when scaling their businesses. Though the cost and effort associated with scaling a mobile business can be significant, careful planning and attention to detail can help create a successful and profitable enterprise that leverages the power of mobile technology.

CONCLUSION:

The smartphone entrepreneur has shown that through careful and smart decision-making, entrepreneurs can use their smartphones to create phenomenal wealth. It has provided a framework of resources and strategies to make the most of the mobile device in pursuit of a profitable online business.

The book has outlined a set of guiding principles, from recognizing the power of the mobile device to understanding the importance of optimizing the digital presence. The key to success lies in making wise and informed decisions—from choosing the right apps and platforms to creating wealth with an innovative and customer-centric approach. Every entrepreneur can use these tactics and strategies to reach their goal of financial stability and economic freedom.

This book has also highlighted the importance of staying connected and being mindful of ever-changing technology. It also stressed the need to develop relationships and maintain a strong social presence. Entrepreneurs can leverage these connections to grow their businesses.

Entrepreneurship is an ever-evolving journey, and The Smartphone Entrepreneur has been an excellent guide. It has polished the vision of these entrepreneurs, allowing them to recognize the potential economic and social impact of their mobile devices.

The Smartphone Entrepreneur has aimed to provide a thorough framework of resources, strategies, and tactics for entrepreneurs to make the most of their smartphones in pursuit of a profitable online business. It has demonstrated how anyone with a mobile device and a dream can use the power of their device to create something out of nothing. It has provided entrepreneurs with an effective platform to monetize their talents and create multiple streams of income. The book has shown that these strategies are simple yet effective.

Smartphone entrepreneurs represent the future of success. Through these entrepreneurial endeavors, anyone can use their own creativity and skills to craft an incredible life. With the resources provided by The Smartphone Entrepreneur, entrepreneurs can have the confidence and strategic power to make the most of their devices and create stunning success stories for generations yet to come.